It's a Feudal, Feudal World

A DIFFERENT Medieval History

Stephen Shapiro

Illustrated by
Ross Kinnaird

annick press
toronto + new york + vancouver

Cover art by Ross Kinnaird
Edited by Alison Kooistra
Designed by Sheryl Shapiro
Proofread by Catherine Marjoribanks

We acknowledge the support of the Canada Council for the Arts, the Ontario Arts Council, and the Government of Canada through the Canada Book Fund (CBF) for our publishing activities.

ONTARIO ARTS COUNCIL
CONSEIL DES ARTS DE L'ONTARIO
50 YEARS OF ONTARIO GOVERNMENT SUPPORT OF THE ARTS
50 ANS DE SOUTIEN DU GOUVERNEMENT DE L'ONTARIO AUX ARTS

Cataloging in Publication

Shapiro, Stephen
   It's a feudal, feudal world : a different medieval history / by Stephen Shapiro ;
illustrated by Ross Kinnaird.

Includes bibliographical references and index. Issued also in electronic format.
ISBN 978-1-55451-553-0 (bound).—ISBN 978-1-55451-552-3 (pbk.)

   1. Civilization, Medieval—Juvenile literature. 2. Middle Ages—
Juvenile literature. I. Kinnaird, Ross, 1954- II. Title. III. Title: It is
a feudal, feudal world.

CB351.S53 2013   j909.07   C2013-901297-4

Distributed in Canada by:
Firefly Books Ltd.
50 Staples Avenue, Unit 1
Richmond Hill, ON L4B 0A7

Published in the U.S.A. by Annick Press (U.S.) Ltd.
Distributed in the U.S.A. by:
Firefly Books (U.S.) Inc.
P.O. Box 1338
Ellicott Station
Buffalo, NY 14205

Printed in China

Visit us at: www.annickpress.com

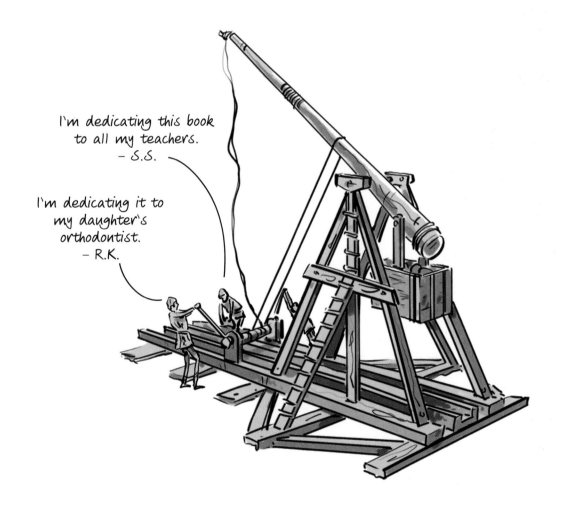

Contents

Introduction

What were the Middle Ages?

The Middle Ages were the thousand years of history in Europe between 500 CE and 1500 CE. This was an age of kings and queens, knights and castles, peasants and plows ...

... but this was also an age of caliphs and khans, longships and librarians, Silk Roads and synagogues. This is a different history of the Middle Ages.

A different history?

Yes. A different history told in a different way—through infographics.

What's an infographic?

An infographic is an image that explains something involving numbers or patterns, like a chart or a diagram.

So, is this an infographic?

0 m (0 feet)   10 m (35 feet)   20 m (70 feet)

Absolutely! So are the pie charts and the timeline on the right.

These pie charts show you the world's population in 1000 CE, halfway through the Middle Ages, and in 2000 CE.

This timeline helps you see where you are in time, compared to the Middle Ages. It also gives you a preview of some of the major events before, during, and after the Middle Ages. As you read on, you may want to flip back to this page to find the events on the timeline.

WORLD POPULATION
1000 CE

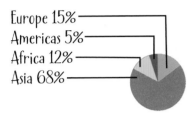

Europe 15%
Americas 5%
Africa 12%
Asia 68%

Total Population: 268 Million

WORLD POPULATION
2000 CE

Europe 12%
Americas 14%
Africa 13%
Asia 61%

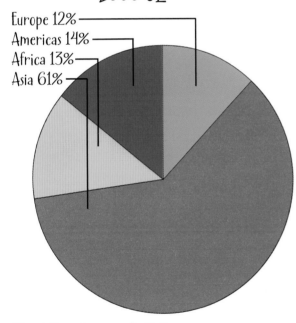

Total Population: 6 Billion

It's called the Middle Ages because it took ages and it's in the middle.
⌐ Just kidding!

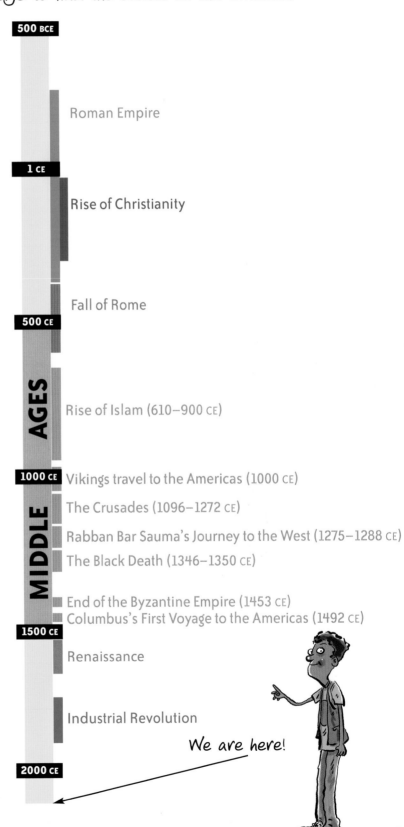

500 BCE

Roman Empire

1 CE

Rise of Christianity

Fall of Rome

500 CE

Rise of Islam (610–900 CE)

1000 CE Vikings travel to the Americas (1000 CE)

The Crusades (1096–1272 CE)

Rabban Bar Sauma's Journey to the West (1275–1288 CE)

The Black Death (1346–1350 CE)

End of the Byzantine Empire (1453 CE)
Columbus's First Voyage to the Americas (1492 CE)

1500 CE

Renaissance

Industrial Revolution

We are here!

2000 CE

The Middle Ages started when the ancient Roman Empire fell. At its peak, the empire included half of Europe as well as parts of Asia, Africa, and the Middle East. In the fifth century, nations from outside the empire moved into Roman Europe and took over, tearing the empire apart and establishing kingdoms of their own.

ASIA

When the empire collapsed, Rome went from being the center of the world to a giant target for looting barbarians. After the city was repeatedly sacked, most Romans decided they'd rather live somewhere else. It took more than a thousand years for Rome's population to get back to its original imperial size!

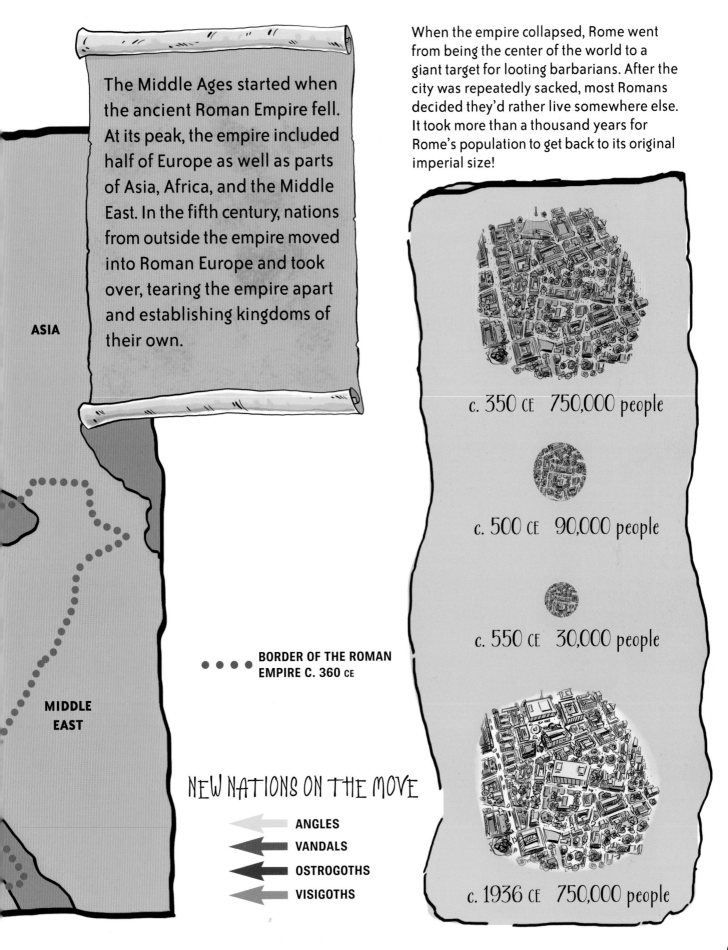

c. 350 CE   750,000 people

c. 500 CE   90,000 people

c. 550 CE   30,000 people

c. 1936 CE   750,000 people

• • • • **BORDER OF THE ROMAN EMPIRE C. 360 CE**

MIDDLE EAST

NEW NATIONS ON THE MOVE

ANGLES
VANDALS
OSTROGOTHS
VISIGOTHS

Three Faiths

The nations that took over the Roman Empire believed in polytheistic (many gods) religions. As the Middle Ages progressed, two monotheistic (one god) religions, Christianity and Islam, split the medieval world between them. Both Christianity and Islam shared stories with an older monotheistic religion, Judaism. At times, these three religions recognized their shared roots as "People of the Book." At other times, they fought each other for control of land, people, and holy sites.

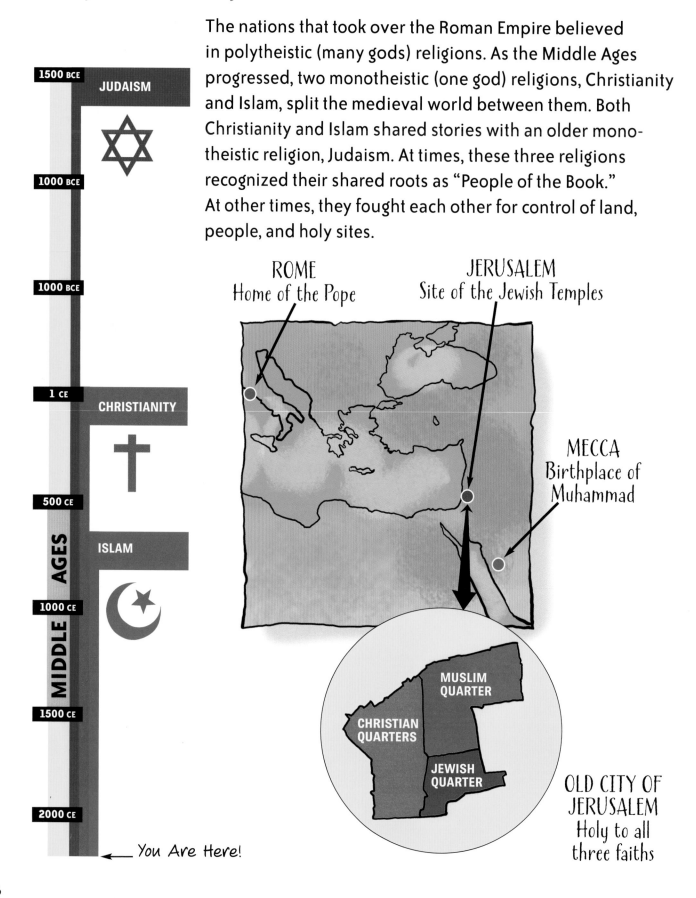

1500 BCE
JUDAISM

1000 BCE

1000 BCE

1 CE
CHRISTIANITY

500 CE

MIDDLE AGES

ISLAM

1000 CE

1500 CE

2000 CE

← You Are Here!

ROME
Home of the Pope

JERUSALEM
Site of the Jewish Temples

MECCA
Birthplace of Muhammad

MUSLIM QUARTER

CHRISTIAN QUARTERS

JEWISH QUARTER

OLD CITY OF JERUSALEM
Holy to all three faiths

ONE GOD, MANY RELIGIONS

Judaism, Christianity, and Islam were all monotheistic religions that originated in the Middle East, but from there they started to diverge. Each had a different holy book, followed different leaders, and built different places to pray.

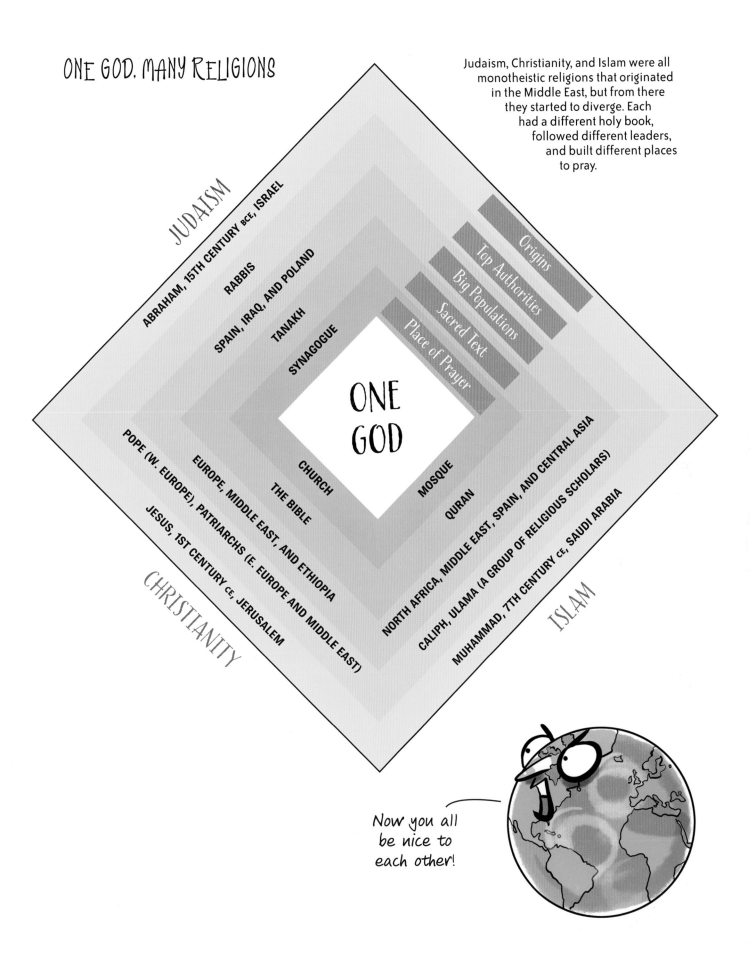

JUDAISM

ABRAHAM, 15TH CENTURY BCE, ISRAEL

RABBIS

SPAIN, IRAQ, AND POLAND

TANAKH

SYNAGOGUE

Origins

Top Authorities

Big Populations

Sacred Text

Place of Prayer

ONE GOD

CHURCH

THE BIBLE

EUROPE, MIDDLE EAST, AND ETHIOPIA

POPE (W. EUROPE), PATRIARCHS (E. EUROPE AND MIDDLE EAST)

JESUS, 1ST CENTURY CE, JERUSALEM

CHRISTIANITY

MOSQUE

QURAN

NORTH AFRICA, MIDDLE EAST, SPAIN, AND CENTRAL ASIA

CALIPH, ULAMA (A GROUP OF RELIGIOUS SCHOLARS)

MUHAMMAD, 7TH CENTURY CE, SAUDI ARABIA

ISLAM

Now you all be nice to each other!

Byzantine Business

The fall of Rome was the end of Roman control over Western Europe. However, the eastern territories of the empire survived with a new capital city, Constantinople. Historians call this eastern empire the Byzantine Empire. The Byzantines had the same amazing diversity as the Romans, but they didn't have the same power. Year after year, the empire shrank.

Why "Byzantine"? Because the empire's capital, Constantinople, used to be called Byzantium.

ROMAN EMPIRE, C. 362 CE ● ● ● ● ● ● ● ● ●
BYZANTINE EMPIRE, C. 555 CE
BYZANTINE EMPIRE, C. 700 CE
BYZANTINE EMPIRE, C. 1071 CE
THE SACK OF CONSTANTINOPLE, 1204 CE
BYZANTINE EMPIRE, C. 1453 CE

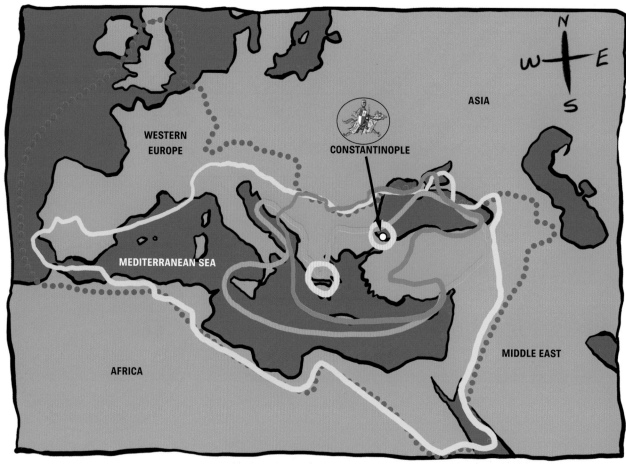

EMPIRE UNDER SIEGE

The Byzantine Empire strikes back, returning Roman law to Italy (c. 555 CE)

I'm not coming to chop wood!

Byzantine Emperor Romanos is captured in battle against the Turks (1071 CE)

Tag. You're it!

I'm the new boss. You got a problem with that?

The new Islamic caliphate (empire) takes control of North Africa and the Middle East (c. 700 CE)

I feel overdressed.

Crusading knights from Western Europe sack Constantinople (1204 CE)

The day is not complete without a bit of besieging.

The Ottoman Empire besieges the Byzantines in Constantinople (1453 CE)

FOLLOW THE MONEY

By counting how many stray coins are found from each era, archaeologists can see when times got bad for the Byzantines. After each crisis, people had less money to spend and held on to their loose change more tightly.

COINS FOUND IN A BYZANTINE CITY

no coins

no coins

| 555 CE | 600 CE | 650 CE | 700 CE | 925 CE | 1000 CE | 1050 CE | 1071 CE | 1204 CE | 1453 CE |

Places of Prayer

In the Middle Ages, every little village had somewhere to pray. But cities also had huge mosques and cathedrals, some of the biggest and most awe-inspiring buildings of the age.

NOTRE-DAME DE REIMS, GOTHIC CATHEDRAL

The thirteenth-century cathedral Notre-Dame de Reims ("Our Lady of Reims") was where the kings and queens of France were crowned.

HEIGHT: 87 m (285 FEET). THIS IS TALLER THAN 14 GIRAFFES!

GREAT MOSQUE OF CORDOBA

Built in 784, the Great Mosque of Cordoba was where the Muslim kings and queens of Spain went to pray.

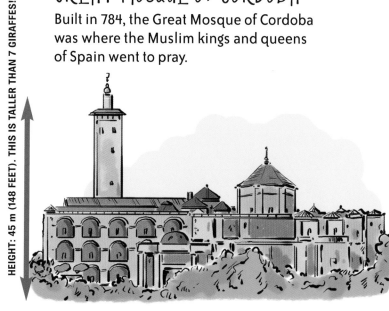

HEIGHT: 45 m (148 FEET). THIS IS TALLER THAN 7 GIRAFFES!

The Notre-Dame de Reims Cathedral was decorated with sculptures representing angels and saints.

40 PILLARS   **2,300 SCULPTURES**

The Mosque of Cordoba had so many pillars it was described as a "forest of stone." Islam forbids putting images of people on mosques, so the Mosque of Cordoba does not have any sculptures. Instead, it is decorated with patterns, flowers, and verses from the Quran.

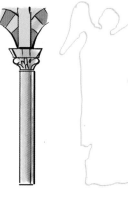

1,013 PILLARS   **0 SCULPTURES**

Flying buttresses keep the walls from exploding under their own weight.

Huge stained-glass windows fill the sanctuary with heavenly light.

Queen Jeanne de Bourbon was crowned on the same day as her husband, King Charles V, but with less ceremony: she came in a side door and had a smaller throne.

Built on top of an older church, which was built on top of Roman baths.

My crown's nicer anyway.

I wish everyone upstairs would be quiet!

NOTRE-DAME DE REIMS, GOTHIC CATHEDRAL
AREA: 4,800 m² (50,000 SQUARE FEET)
THIS IS A BIT BIGGER THAN A FOOTBALL FIELD!

GREAT MOSQUE OF CORDOBA
AREA: 24,000 m² (260,000 SQUARE FEET)
THIS IS BIGGER THAN 5 FOOTBALL FIELDS!

The minaret was climbed five times a day to call the faithful to prayer.

You can really lose yourself in there!

Columns taken from nearby Roman ruins.

The mihrab shows people which direction to face when they pray.

Built on the foundations of a church.

Viking Voyages

The Vikings started out in Scandinavia (in Northern Europe), but they didn't stay put. The word "Viking" means "to go overseas" in Old Norse, the Viking language. They raided villages wherever they went, stealing money and food and destroying buildings. In some cases, they overthrew the local kings and took power for themselves. But they also traded and settled, making Viking villages just like the ones at home.

Fearsome longships carried the Vikings on swift raids that terrorized people all across Europe.

Now I'm really going to be late for school!

How big was a longship?

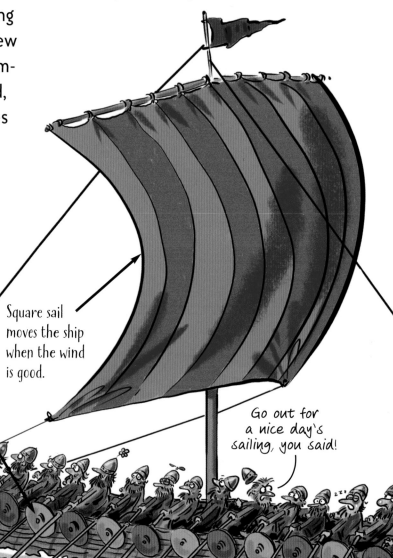

Shields protect the rowers from waves and arrows.

Square sail moves the ship when the wind is good.

Long, narrow hull is fast in the water.

Steering oar guides the ship.

Go out for a nice day's sailing, you said!

Oars let the Vikings move the ship when there is no wind, or when the wind is coming from the wrong direction.

Why didn't we settle in Florida?

Viking settlers started villages in Iceland (nice and green) and Greenland (just frozen ice), and even sailed all the way to Newfoundland.

Swap some old dried cod for some vodka?

Meh.

In Russia, Viking traders helped found the city of Kiev in 882 CE.

The queen is not going to be happy about this.

Viking warriors conquered kingdoms in England, Normandy, and southern Italy.

WHERE DID THE VIKINGS GO?

874 CE: ICELAND

882 CE: RUSSIA

911 CE: NORMANDY

985 CE: GREENLAND

1000 CE: CANADA

1030 CE: ITALY

1066 CE: ENGLAND

Dragon head terrifies enemies.

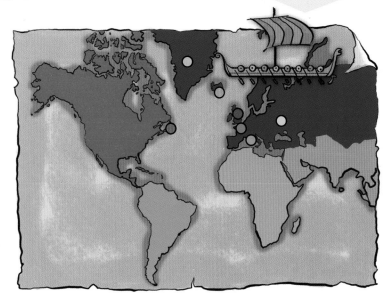

On the Road

It was tough to get around when nothing moved faster than a horse, but there were still all sorts of people on the roads in the Middle Ages. There were messengers carrying urgent letters, diplomats bringing offers of alliance, clerics preaching their religion, and merchants carrying goods to sell, plus pilgrims heading to and from holy places. Just a big medieval traffic jam!

(Want to know more about merchants and traders? See pages 30–33.)

When you visit someone, it's only polite to bring a gift. In 802 CE, Arab ambassadors visiting the Frankish emperor Charlemagne gave him an elephant. The first elephant in Europe in a thousand years, it made a big splash ... literally: the elephant died eight years later from a cold it got from swimming in the Rhine River.

Ta-da!

Did you keep the receipt?

TRAVELING: HOW FAR IN A DAY?

WALKING

PILGRIM 32 km (20 MILES)

RIDING A CAMEL

MERCHANT 40 km (25 MILES)

RIDING A HORSE

DIPLOMAT 56 km (35 MILES)

GETTING A NEW HORSE WHEN THE LAST ONE GETS TIRED

MESSENGER 72 km (45 MILES)

ROWING

RAIDER 152 km (95 MILES)

SAILING

TRADER 192 km (120 MILES)

It took me a whole year to walk from Iraq to Germany!

ELEPHANT 80 km (50 MILES)

The Mongol emperor and empress enjoyed inviting travelers to stay at their court and share their different views on religion.

What is the best way to live?

CHRISTIANITY
TO WORSHIP GOD AND FOLLOW THE TEACHINGS OF GOD'S SON, JESUS, WHO DIED FOR OUR SINS.

SHAMANISM
TO HONOR THE SPIRITS THAT SURROUND US AND REACH OUT TO THEM FOR GUIDANCE AND HEALING.

ISLAM
TO SUBMIT TO THE WILL OF GOD AND FOLLOW THE TEACHINGS OF MUHAMMAD, GOD'S LAST AND MOST PERFECT PROPHET.

BUDDHISM
TO ABANDON ALL EARTHLY DESIRES AND SEEK ENLIGHTENMENT.

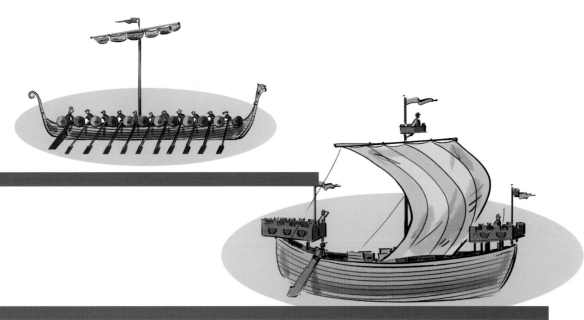

It's a Feudal, Feudal World

The Middle Ages were a dangerous time, with kings and queens going to war for land, for power, and for religion. If you had to fight a guy with a big sword, you needed a guy with a big sword! But how did you pay him without money? "Feudalism" was the system that allowed nobles to use their land to create armies of knights. It all goes like this:

omg!

The king or queen gives land (a fief) to a noble (their vassal) in exchange for their service.

wow!

The noble gives some of the land to a lower-ranked noble and makes them a vassal.

thx

The lower-ranked noble gives a bit of land to a knight, making him a vassal.

Faster! This horse is already obsolete ...

Peasants farm the knight's land. They pay "rent" by giving him some of the food they grow each year. The knight uses this income to pay for a horse and armor.

When the king or queen goes to war, they summon their vassals. The vassals bring their vassals, giving the king or queen the army they need.

I'm confused too.

BUT
In the real world, vassals often held land from several different lords and sometimes granted fiefs to people who were also lords themselves. It was possible to be both the lord and the vassal of the same person!

Feudalism was a European system. But similar systems of trading land for loyalty and service existed all over the medieval world.

IF YOU OWNED A FIEF, YOU:

LIVED: somewhere in Western Europe, like England or France

GOT THE LAND FROM: a lord, for as long as you lived

GOT CONTROL OF: people and land

HAD TO: fight for the lord as a knight

IF YOU OWNED AN ALLOD, YOU:

LIVED: somewhere in Central or Eastern Europe, like Germany or Poland

GOT THE LAND FROM: a parent or relative, for as long as you lived

GOT CONTROL OF: people and land

HAD TO: be nice to your family

IF YOU OWNED A PRONOIA, YOU:

LIVED: somewhere in the Byzantine Empire (see pages 8–9), like Greece or Turkey

GOT THE LAND FROM: the emperor, for as long as the emperor let you keep it

GOT CONTROL OF: rent money from peasants working your land

HAD TO: obey the emperor's laws

IF YOU OWNED A TIMAR OR IQTA, YOU:

LIVED: somewhere in an Islamic empire, like Egypt or Syria

GOT THE LAND FROM: a lord, for as long as the lord let you keep it

GOT CONTROL OF: tax money from people living on your land

HAD TO: fight for the lord

Maniacs on Horseback

The knight was the super-weapon of medieval warfare, but he was not unstoppable. All it took was good tactics and the willingness to get in the way of several tons of hurtling horseman, and he ...

He?

Don't forget, there were some women who fought as knights. Joan of Arc, Isabel of Conches, Aethelflaed of Mercia, Joanna of Flanders ...

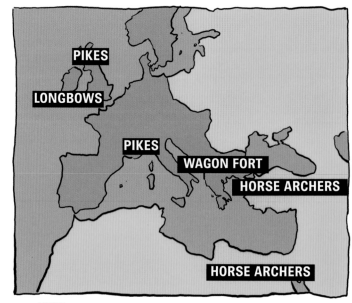

HERE BE THERE KNIGHTS

WHEN A KNIGHT CHARGES:

The horse gallops forward at 500 metres (547 yards) a minute.

The lance comes up, steadied in the knight's armpit in the "couched" position.

Don't mess with her.

MOBILITY   DEFENSE   FIREPOWER

The stirrups and high-backed saddle absorb the impact.

Different armies developed different strategies for fighting against knights.

PIKES

MOBILITY   **DEFENSE**   **FIREPOWER**

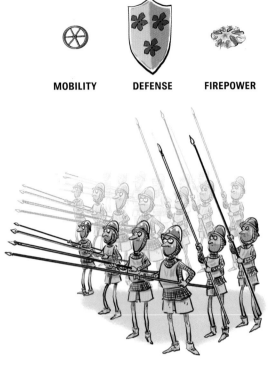

Pikes provide soldiers with 360° protection, as long as the soldiers stay close together.

LONGBOWS

MOBILITY   **DEFENSE**   **FIREPOWER**

Wooden stakes in front of the archers trip up oncoming knights. Arrows from longbows can skewer a knight or horse 400 metres (437 yards) away.

WAGON FORT

MOBILITY   **DEFENSE**   **FIREPOWER**

Wagons and spears block enemy charges. Bows and cannons blast oncoming knights.

HORSE ARCHERS

MOBILITY   **DEFENSE**   **FIREPOWER**

Swift horses dodge charging knights. The archers can shoot at weak spots like a knight's back or side.

Food and Farms

In the Middle Ages, food wasn't just as good as gold—it was better. What else could you eat for breakfast or use to pay your rent? Here's what people grew and ate in Northern Europe.

Peasants mostly ate barley bread and beer, with pork, chicken, and cheese as occasional luxuries.

Lords and ladies ate wheat bread and plenty of meat—and not just beef, chicken, and pork. Nobles also hunted deer and birds for sport.

YOU ARE WHERE YOU EAT

What medieval people ate, and how they prepared their food, was affected by what kinds of plants could grow in their local climate.

No grapes? Ferment grain to make beer.

No olives? Grease your pot with animal fat.

Lots of vines? Crush grapes and make wine.

You're in luck! Use olive oil to fry up your food.

Thirsty? Ferment figs for a tasty drink.

COOL   WARM

MILD   HOT

AN ENGLISH FARMING VILLAGE

Yo, dudes, that's my hood!

1 Peasant homes (made mostly of wood and straw)

2 The lord's manor house (usually the only house made of stone in the village)

3 The village church (for prayer, marriages, and keeping records)

4 Fields of crops (organized in long strips, so that plows didn't have to make many turns)

CHANGING CROPS

Many medieval farmers divided their fields into thirds, switching which crops they grew in each field from year to year. In England and France, they grew:

2 Legumes (peas and beans)
* Have protein
* Add nitrogen to the soil but remove minerals

Listen up ... Changing crops keeps the soil rich and fertile.

1 Grains (wheat and barley)
* Are good for making bread and beer, important peasant foods
* Remove lots of nitrogen and minerals from the soil

3 Unplanted ("fallow")
* Lets the soil recover the nitrogen and minerals that help crops grow

Growing Up

For a medieval kid, life was cruel and dangerous. Only the lucky survived, but being born into a rich family was a good start.

Without modern medicine, every birth was dangerous for mother and child.

I know best, I'm THE DOCTOR!

Phew! I made it!

I know best, I'm THE MIDWIFE!

DOCTORS
* Trained in a university or guild
* Followed centuries-old medical textbooks
* Never touched a woman except in emergencies
* Hired by nobles and rich merchants
* Chances of Success: So-So

MIDWIVES
* Trained by practice and apprenticeship
* Followed traditions passed down through generations
* Provided hands-on help during births
* Hired by peasants and artisans
* Chances of Success: So-So

THE DEADLY HOME

The home of a medieval peasant was a deadly place for the average infant. Among the dangers in and around the home were:

4% died from crumbling walls

The strangest cause of death? 5% died from pig bites

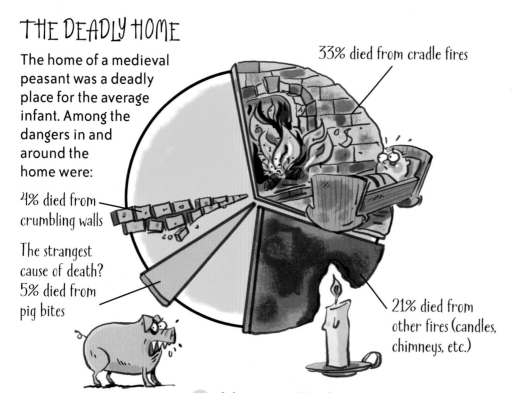

33% died from cradle fires

21% died from other fires (candles, chimneys, etc.)

Other causes of death

THE DEADLIEST SEASON

The most dangerous time of year was the harvest, a month when the entire village was working in the fields and no one was at home watching the babies.

47%

of all infant deaths happened during the harvest.

If you survived childhood, the odds got better. Those who reached the age of 20 had a 50% chance of living another 30 or so years. (In North America today, the average life expectancy is 80 years.)

| 12 | 13 | 14 | 15 | 16 | 17 | 18 | 19 | 20 | 21 | 22 | 23 | 24 | 25 | 26 | 27 |

NOBILITY

Young nobles learned how to be a lady or knight by serving an older one as a lady-in-waiting or squire. They ran errands, helped their mistress or master dress, and learned how to act like a noble. Many married young because marriages brought land and alliances.

Go Into Service   Get Married   Knighted (men)

ARTISANS

Artisans were tradespeople like bakers, weavers, carpenters, and blacksmiths. Young people became apprentices by going to live with someone who had mastered one of these crafts and learning their trade.

Become Apprentice   Graduate   Get Married

PEASANTRY

The life of a young peasant was like that of an old peasant, just poorer. Most worked as farmers; others washed clothes for nobles or worked as household servants. Most couldn't afford to marry until later in life.

Go to Work   Get Married

AGE   12 13 14 15 16 17 18 19 20 21 22 23 24 25 26 27

The Daily Grind

Before anyone invented the factory or the office, medieval workers were busy making iron, cloth, wine, and all sorts of other things. Workers called "artisans" specialized in different products and organized themselves into groups called "guilds."

Each guild was a pyramid: hardworking apprentices could become journeymen, and talented journeymen could become masters. Despite the title, not all journeymen were men: silk and lace guilds were often all women, and wives often worked in or managed their husbands' workshops.

I hate heights.

Every town had a mix of different trades. In the great German city of Frankfurt the mix looked like this:

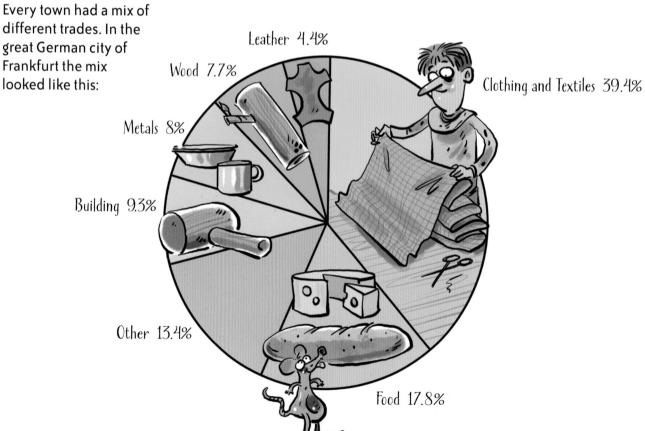

Leather 4.4%

Wood 7.7%

Metals 8%

Building 9.3%

Other 13.4%

Clothing and Textiles 39.4%

Food 17.8%

Medieval workers used all sorts of machines to make goods, but the most important was the gristmill, which turned grain into flour for bread.

MILLS WERE POWERED IN DIFFERENT WAYS:

Animal Power
HORSE

Animal motion rotates center pole to drive millstone

HOW THE GRISTMILL WORKS

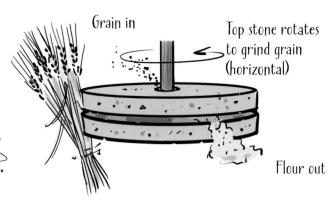

Grain in

Top stone rotates to grind grain (horizontal)

Flour out

Primitive Water Power
UNDERSHOT WATERWHEEL

Gears change vertical rotation to horizontal to drive millstone

Water rotates wheel

Advanced Water Power
OVERSHOT WATERWHEEL

Weight of water rotates wheel with more power

Gears change vertical rotation to horizontal to drive millstone

Wind Power
WINDMILL

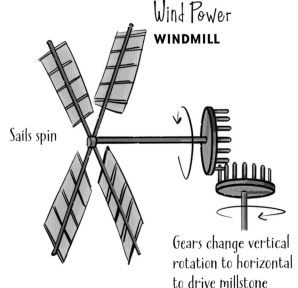

Sails spin

Gears change vertical rotation to horizontal to drive millstone

FLOUR PRODUCTION

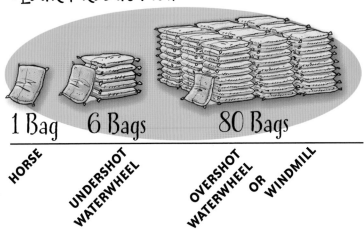

1 Bag — HORSE

6 Bags — UNDERSHOT WATERWHEEL

80 Bags — OVERSHOT WATERWHEEL OR WINDMILL

Ladies and Linen-workers

Noble women had a lot of influence. Some were rulers themselves, while others were leaders of the court, diplomats, and patrons of the arts. For women who weren't rich, the work never ended. In addition to cooking, cleaning, and child-watching, most women worked in their families' businesses, and many had their own professions.

In some towns, there were women-only guilds that made yarn, silk, linen, and gold thread.

WOMEN WORKING

In Paris, where 15% of taxpaying workers were women, most of them worked in a few particular jobs:

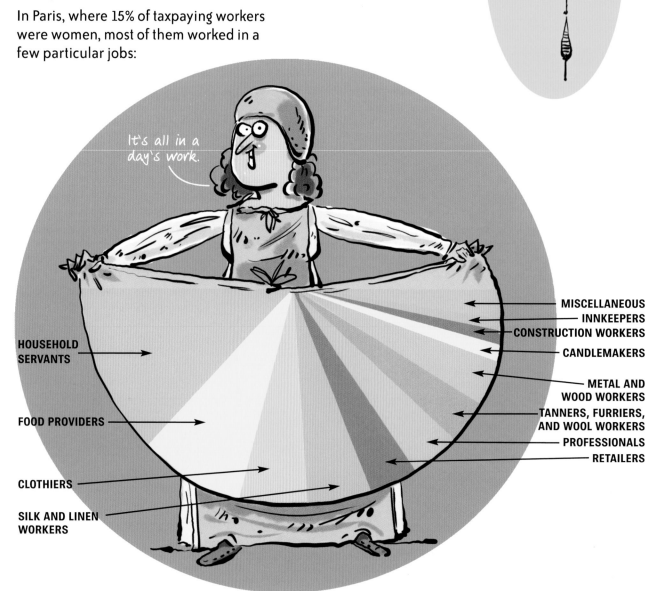

It's all in a day's work.

HOUSEHOLD SERVANTS

FOOD PROVIDERS

CLOTHIERS

SILK AND LINEN WORKERS

MISCELLANEOUS
INNKEEPERS
CONSTRUCTION WORKERS
CANDLEMAKERS
METAL AND WOOD WORKERS
TANNERS, FURRIERS, AND WOOL WORKERS
PROFESSIONALS
RETAILERS

WOMEN RULING

One of the most powerful women in the Middle Ages was Eleanor of Aquitaine (1122–1204). Eleanor helped to lead the Second Crusade, bringing thousands of her vassals to fight the war and 300 noblewomen to help tend to the wounded. When she returned to France, she invited the best poets and musicians to stay at her court and supported them financially.

WOMEN WRITING

Rich patrons like Eleanor of Aquitaine made it possible for talented people to make writing their job. The chart below shows the paths of some of the most famous medieval women writers.

ELEANOR OF AQUITAINE

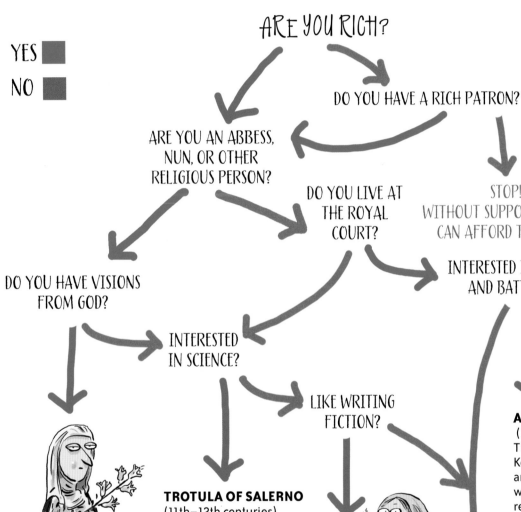

YES ■
NO ■

ARE YOU RICH?

DO YOU HAVE A RICH PATRON?

ARE YOU AN ABBESS, NUN, OR OTHER RELIGIOUS PERSON?

DO YOU LIVE AT THE ROYAL COURT?

STOP!
WITHOUT SUPPORT, NO ONE CAN AFFORD TO WRITE

DO YOU HAVE VISIONS FROM GOD?

INTERESTED IN SCIENCE?

INTERESTED IN WARS AND BATTLES?

LIKE WRITING FICTION?

ANNA KOMNENE
(11th–12th centuries)
The Byzantine princess Anna Komnene studied philosophy and used the palace archives to write a history of her father's reign as emperor, which she called the Alexiad.

TROTULA OF SALERNO
(11th–12th centuries)
A doctor living in southern Italy, Trotula wrote some of Europe's first medical textbooks using information from Arabic, Jewish, and Roman sources.

CATHERINE OF SIENA
(14th century)
While living a religious life of silence and solitude, Catherine had a vision that inspired her to travel Italy preaching total love for God. Her Dialogue of Divine Providence describes a soul's progress towards God.

MARIE DE FRANCE
(12th century)
A French poet living in England, Marie wrote lais (stories on romance and adventure) full of knights, magic, monsters, and forbidden love.

WALLADAH BINT AL-MUSTAKFI
(11th century)
Walladah was a princess from Islamic Spain who wrote poems about her life and her romances. She became famous for competing in poetry contests, stitching verses onto her sleeves, and teaching poetry to women from all social classes.

By the Book

Knowledge grew slowly in the Middle Ages because books and teachers were rare. Some librarians chained the books to the shelves so no one could run off with them!

MATERIALS

No one knows exactly how much of the population could read or write, but even rich nobles often needed to hire scribes to write letters for them. And there was another catch: no paper. So people used animal skins, reeds, and tree trunks:

Parchment

👍 **VERY DURABLE**

👎 **SKIN MAY HAVE VEINS OR SCARS**

Papyrus

👍 **EASY TO MAKE**

👎 **REEDS ONLY GROW IN AFRICA**

Bark

👍 **EXTREMELY CHEAP**

👎 **HARD TO WRITE ON**

MARGINALIA

Books were rare because they had to be copied by hand. In Europe, the copying was done by monks, who got bored and doodled in the margins.

now I've written the whole thing, so give me a drink

this parchment is hairy

oh, my hand

A ROYAL LIBRARY

What was King Edward III of England (1312–1377 CE) reading?

68 religious books
23%

160 miscellaneous books
53%

11 law books
4%

59 adventure stories
20%

How to be a long ruler

THE PRINTING PRESS

Books only became numerous after Johannes Gutenberg invented the modern printing press in 1460 CE. China and Korea already had presses, but it was Gutenberg who put all the parts together to make book-making faster.

1 Metal Type
HOT METAL IS POURED INTO THE MOLD TO MAKE EACH LETTER

2 Movable Type
REARRANGING LETTERS LETS THE PRINTERS MAKE ANY WORD

3 Printing Press
PRESSING LETTERS COVERED IN INK AGAINST PAPER CREATES A BOOK

4 The Book

TA DA!

Goods and Gold

People who lived in Europe had wool, but no cotton; people who lived in Africa had cotton, but no wool.

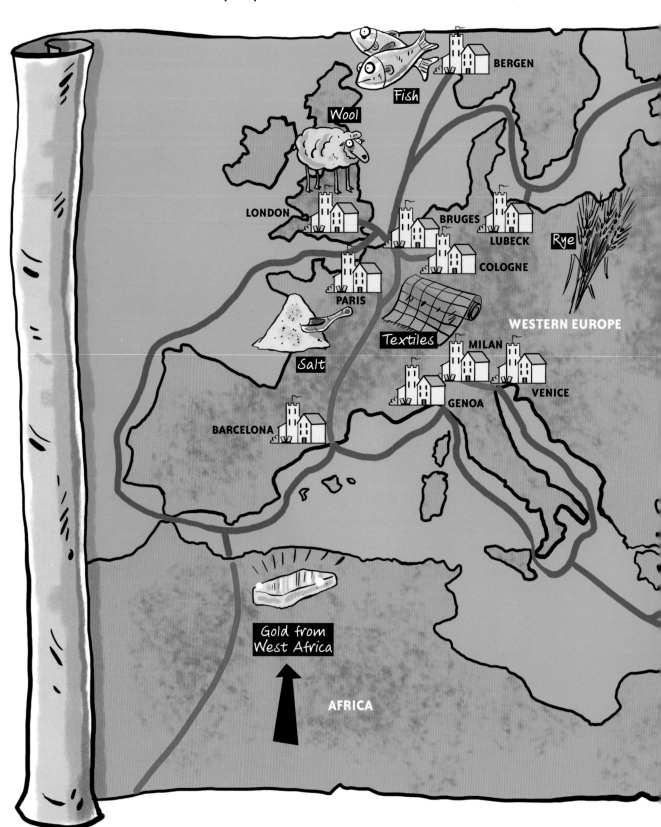

Crisscrossing the medieval world, merchants made their money bringing objects people wanted from one market town to the next.

The Silk Road

Some merchants went all the way from Europe to China and back, carrying luxury goods like silk. Their route—the Silk Road—was used by preachers and diplomats too.

You could buy pretty much *anything* in a Silk Road market:

Is that good-quality dung?

I made it myself.

Cartload of dung
22 coins

Turkish horse
10,000 coins

Roll of silk
510 coins

Pound of cinnamon
96 coins

Pound of sandalwood perfume
1,812 coins

A TURKISH HORSE COST THE SAME AS:

5.5 pounds of sandalwood perfume

20 rolls of silk

104 pounds of cinnamon or

455 cartloads of dung!

It took months or even years to go between Europe and China. Two of the most famous Silk Road travelers were Marco Polo and Rabban Bar Sauma.

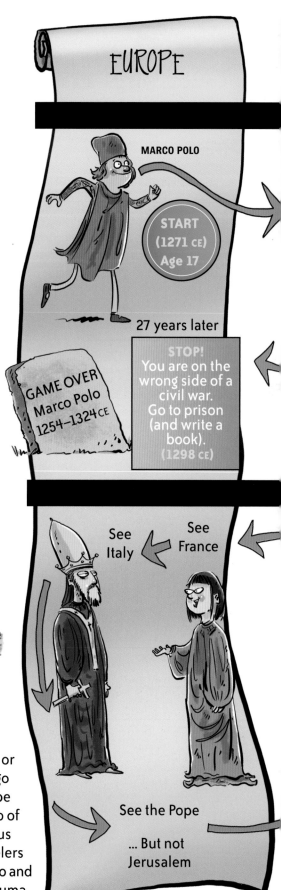

EUROPE

MARCO POLO

START
(1271 CE)
Age 17

27 years later

STOP!
You are on the wrong side of a civil war.
Go to prison (and write a book).
(1298 CE)

GAME OVER
Marco Polo
1254–1324 CE

See France

See Italy

See the Pope

... But not Jerusalem

PERSIA

CENTRAL ASIA

CHINA

Marco Polo was an Italian silk trader who turned the story of his journey into Europe's first great travel story.

EMPEROR KUBLAI KHAN

MISSION:
Trade silk and get rich

Forget about going home— I want you to stay here!

Sail home with riches and treasures

Miss a turn for 17 years

Rabban Bar Sauma was a Christian monk from China whose pilgrimage to Jerusalem turned into a tour of Europe.

EMPEROR ARGHUN

RABBAN BAR SAUMA

START (1275 CE) Age 52

MISSION:
Visit the holy city of Jerusalem

Forget your pilgrimage— go to Europe as my diplomat!

13 years later

STOP! And write a book about your adventures. (1288 CE)

GAME OVER Rabban Bar Sauma 1223–1294 CE

The Crusades

When Pope Urban II called on Europe's Christians to go conquer Jerusalem in 1096, thousands of knights went on the warpath to take the city from the Muslims who lived there. The Crusaders tried for two hundred years, but they never gained lasting control of Jerusalem ...

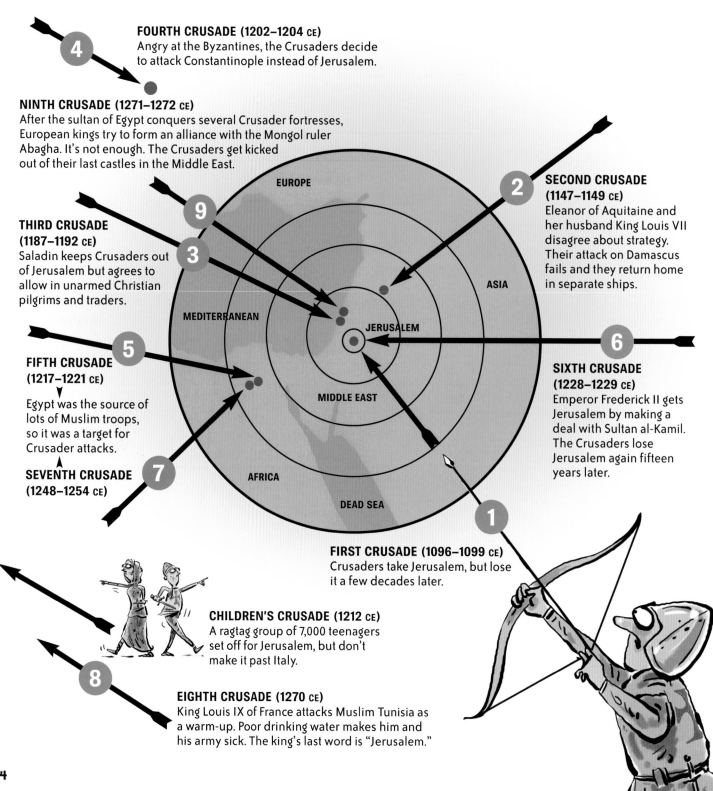

FOURTH CRUSADE (1202–1204 CE)
Angry at the Byzantines, the Crusaders decide to attack Constantinople instead of Jerusalem.

NINTH CRUSADE (1271–1272 CE)
After the sultan of Egypt conquers several Crusader fortresses, European kings try to form an alliance with the Mongol ruler Abagha. It's not enough. The Crusaders get kicked out of their last castles in the Middle East.

THIRD CRUSADE (1187–1192 CE)
Saladin keeps Crusaders out of Jerusalem but agrees to allow in unarmed Christian pilgrims and traders.

SECOND CRUSADE (1147–1149 CE)
Eleanor of Aquitaine and her husband King Louis VII disagree about strategy. Their attack on Damascus fails and they return home in separate ships.

EUROPE

ASIA

MEDITERRANEAN

JERUSALEM

FIFTH CRUSADE (1217–1221 CE)
Egypt was the source of lots of Muslim troops, so it was a target for Crusader attacks.

SEVENTH CRUSADE (1248–1254 CE)

MIDDLE EAST

SIXTH CRUSADE (1228–1229 CE)
Emperor Frederick II gets Jerusalem by making a deal with Sultan al-Kamil. The Crusaders lose Jerusalem again fifteen years later.

AFRICA

DEAD SEA

FIRST CRUSADE (1096–1099 CE)
Crusaders take Jerusalem, but lose it a few decades later.

CHILDREN'S CRUSADE (1212 CE)
A ragtag group of 7,000 teenagers set off for Jerusalem, but don't make it past Italy.

EIGHTH CRUSADE (1270 CE)
King Louis IX of France attacks Muslim Tunisia as a warm-up. Poor drinking water makes him and his army sick. The king's last word is "Jerusalem."

CRUSADER CASTLES

The Crusaders built huge castles to control their new territories. At Krak des Chevaliers in Syria, 60 knights held off thousands of attackers for a month!

A month? It felt like a year!

WAYS TO CONQUER A CASTLE

WAYS TO DEFEND A CASTLE

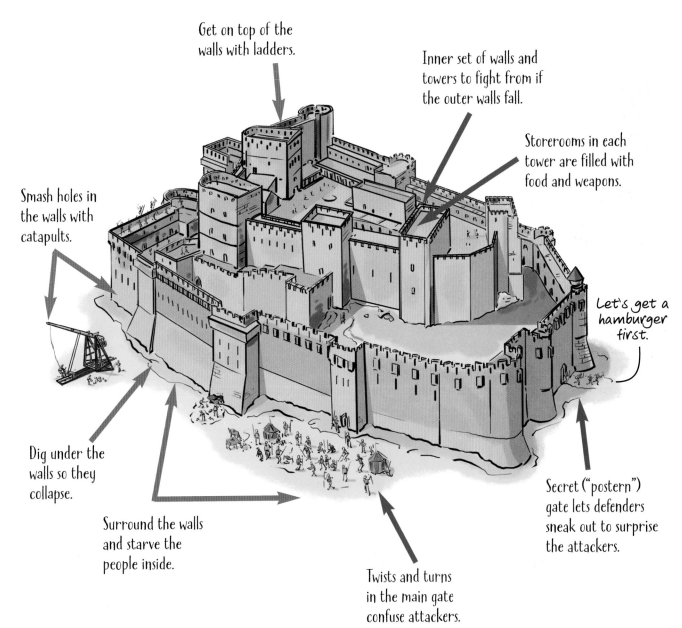

Get on top of the walls with ladders.

Smash holes in the walls with catapults.

Dig under the walls so they collapse.

Surround the walls and starve the people inside.

Inner set of walls and towers to fight from if the outer walls fall.

Storerooms in each tower are filled with food and weapons.

Let's get a hamburger first.

Secret ("postern") gate lets defenders sneak out to surprise the attackers.

Twists and turns in the main gate confuse attackers.

Perilous Persecutions

Sometimes, being different was dangerous. Worshiping a different god, praying in a different way, or wearing different clothes could be deadly. In medieval Spain, minorities had four choices: convert to the dominant religion, pretend to convert and practice your faith in secret, leave town, or stay—and watch your back.

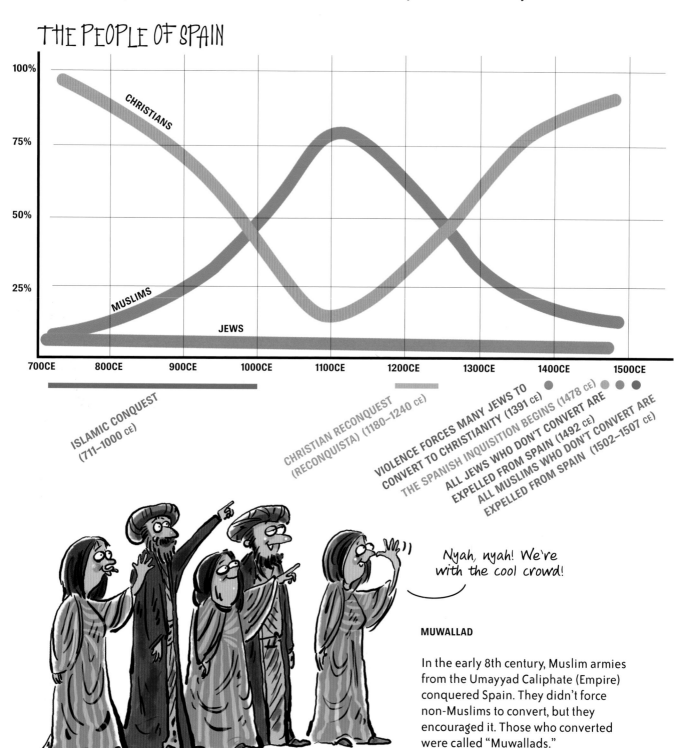

THE PEOPLE OF SPAIN

CHRISTIANS

MUSLIMS

JEWS

ISLAMIC CONQUEST (711–1000 CE)

CHRISTIAN RECONQUEST (RECONQUISTA) (1180–1240 CE)

VIOLENCE FORCES MANY JEWS TO CONVERT TO CHRISTIANITY (1391 CE)

THE SPANISH INQUISITION BEGINS (1478 CE)

ALL JEWS WHO DON'T CONVERT ARE EXPELLED FROM SPAIN (1492 CE)

ALL MUSLIMS WHO DON'T CONVERT ARE EXPELLED FROM SPAIN (1502–1507 CE)

Nyah, nyah! We're with the cool crowd!

MUWALLAD

In the early 8th century, Muslim armies from the Umayyad Caliphate (Empire) conquered Spain. They didn't force non-Muslims to convert, but they encouraged it. Those who converted were called "Muwallads."

Muslim caliphs respected Christians and Jews as "People of the Book," since all three faiths share some of the same sacred stories. But they also made rules for those who kept their religion instead of converting. They were called "Dhimmis."

Christian kingdoms tried for centuries to reconquer Spain. In the 12th century, the tide turned in their favor. Once in control, they made rules for Muslims who stayed in Spain but did not convert to Christianity. These people were called "Mudejars."

At the end of the 15th century, the king and queen demanded that all citizens either convert to Christianity or leave the country. Jews who converted to Christianity were called "Conversos" and Muslims who converted were called "Moriscoes."

Enforcers called "Inquisitors" were sent out to find people practicing Judaism or Islam in secret. Inquisitors imprisoned or tortured people until they confessed. Lucky ones might only be fined. The worst punishment was to be burned at the stake.

8TH CENTURY

The rules were:
* Wear a coarse rope belt, the "zunnar"
* Don't pray in public
* Don't build new churches or synagogues
* Pay a special tax, the "jizya"
* Don't carry weapons
* Don't marry Muslims

12TH CENTURY

The rules were:
* Wear clothing marked with a blue crescent
* Don't pray in public
* Don't build mosques
* Pay an extra tax, the "besant"
* Don't mix with Christians
* Listen to sermons from Christian priests

15TH CENTURY

If you did any of the following things, your neighbor might turn you in to the Inquisitors as somebody

... who might secretly be Jewish:
* Didn't eat pork
* Lit candles on Friday night
* Didn't work on Saturday (the Jewish Sabbath)
* Hung out with people who were known to be Jewish

I just don't suit rope.

And whenever something goes wrong, I get blamed!

DHIMMI

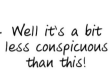
Well it's a bit less conspicuous than this!

And whenever something goes wrong, I get blamed!

MUDEJAR

Uh oh! Here come the Inquisitors!

And whenever something goes wrong, I get blamed!

MORISCO

No BLT for me, please!

CONVERSO

... who might secretly be Muslim:
* Didn't eat pork or drink wine
* Didn't eat during the day during Ramadan (an Islamic festival)
* Bathed on Fridays
* Spoke or read Arabic

The Big, Bad Black Death

The bubonic plague was bad news. All it took was a tiny flea bite and you broke out in black bulges (or buboes) and died. No medicine could stop it. Flea bites and the bacteria they passed to a person were too small for medieval doctors to see, so they thought the disease was caused by a kind of bad air they called a "miasma."

THE PLAGUE SPREAD

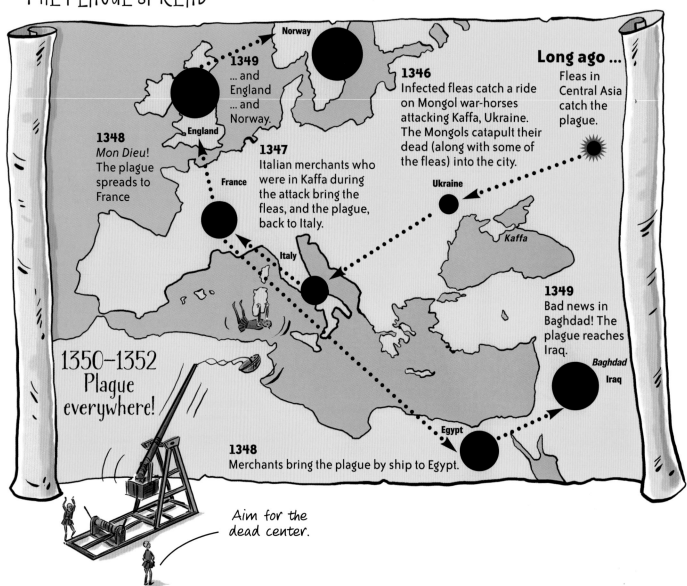

Long ago ...
Fleas in Central Asia catch the plague.

1346
Infected fleas catch a ride on Mongol war-horses attacking Kaffa, Ukraine. The Mongols catapult their dead (along with some of the fleas) into the city.

1347
Italian merchants who were in Kaffa during the attack bring the fleas, and the plague, back to Italy.

1348
Mon Dieu! The plague spreads to France

1349
... and England ... and Norway.

1349
Bad news in Baghdad! The plague reaches Iraq.

1348
Merchants bring the plague by ship to Egypt.

1350–1352
Plague everywhere!

The fleas carrying the plague traveled in the fur of rats. From the rats, the fleas jumped to other bodies ... human ones. When the plague arrived in Europe, it killed almost two-thirds of the population in just a few years. But some groups of people were less likely to die than others.

Eeeew! Like I'm so over this plague thing.

People who were rich—like nobles—were less likely to die than people who were poor—like orphans. This was because poor people lived in crowded housing and were too weak to fight off a tough disease.

Monks did well because they lived away from cities and towns, but once the plague got into the monastery everyone was at risk.

WHO DIED?

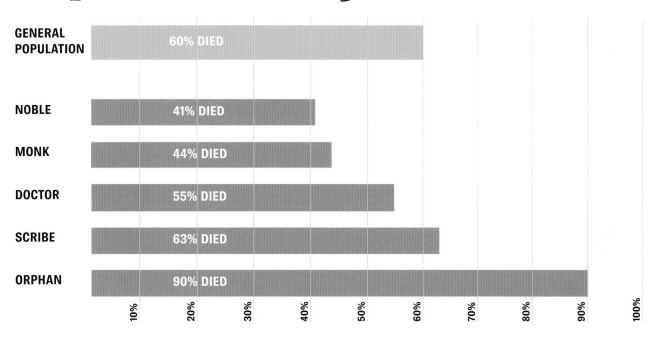

GENERAL POPULATION	60% DIED
NOBLE	41% DIED
MONK	44% DIED
DOCTOR	55% DIED
SCRIBE	63% DIED
ORPHAN	90% DIED

10% 20% 30% 40% 50% 60% 70% 80% 90% 100%

Write it yourself!

Scribes were at risk because they were often called on to write out wills for those who were sick.

Ooooh! Thank you for coming, Doctor.

Although doctors were rich and well fed, they frequently caught the plague from fleas in their patients' homes.

How Did the Middle Ages End?

In the fifteenth and sixteenth centuries the big symbols of the Middle Ages started to vanish. Knights and castles disappeared, cities grew by leaps and bounds, and the Church began to change. What happened?

- Gunpowder from China led to the invention of new weapons that blew up the power of the knights (literally!).

- Sailors like Christopher Columbus and Vasco da Gama found new routes to travel that gave the medieval world access to new ideas, foods, products, lands, and wealth.

- New ideas and ways to spread them sparked revolutions in science and religion that created new technologies and challenged the power of the Church.

The feudal, feudal world was gone forever.

SOURCES OF CHANGE

START

Feudal knights divide up kingdoms among themselves.

GUNPOWDER
Cannons let monarchs blast away at knights' castles.

Who's going to mow the lawn?

I'd like a hammock in the corner.

Monarchs reign supreme

END

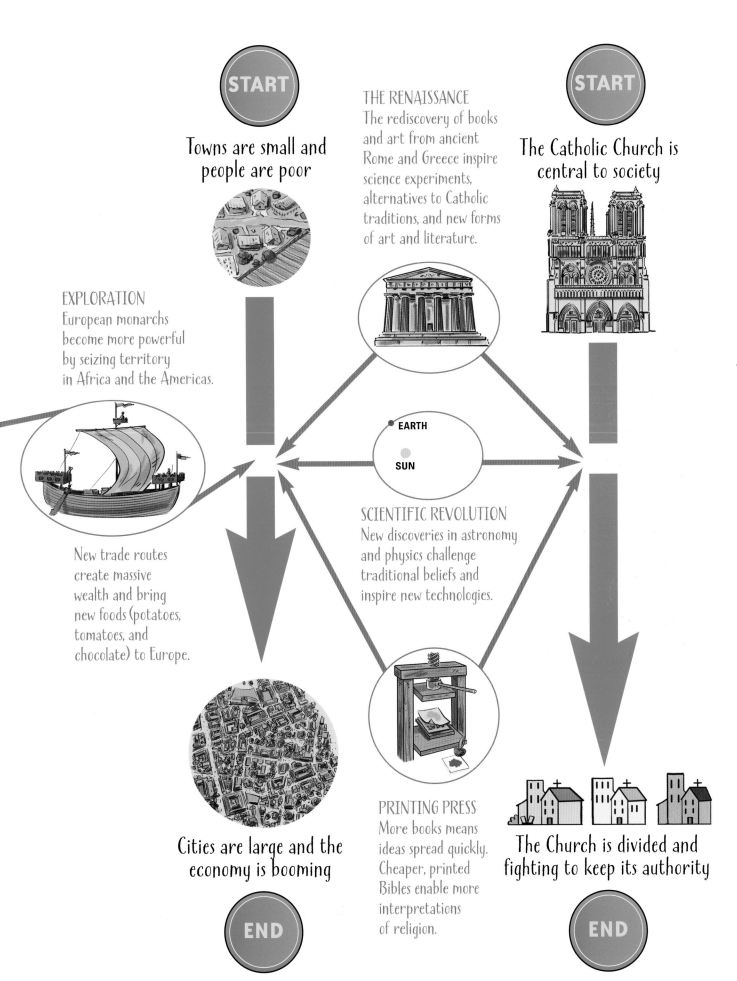

START

Towns are small and people are poor

THE RENAISSANCE
The rediscovery of books and art from ancient Rome and Greece inspire science experiments, alternatives to Catholic traditions, and new forms of art and literature.

START

The Catholic Church is central to society

EXPLORATION
European monarchs become more powerful by seizing territory in Africa and the Americas.

EARTH

SUN

New trade routes create massive wealth and bring new foods (potatoes, tomatoes, and chocolate) to Europe.

SCIENTIFIC REVOLUTION
New discoveries in astronomy and physics challenge traditional beliefs and inspire new technologies.

Cities are large and the economy is booming

PRINTING PRESS
More books means ideas spread quickly. Cheaper, printed Bibles enable more interpretations of religion.

The Church is divided and fighting to keep its authority

END

END

GLOSSARY

apprentice
a person who learns a skill or trade from an older, more established worker.

archaeologist
a person who studies the objects left behind by past cultures—everything from pyramids to huts, art to money, and skeletons to cooking pots.

artisan
a skilled craftsperson who works with their hands to make a product. Different kinds of artisans make different kinds of products—anything from bread, to jewelry, to furniture, to clothing, to weapons.

BCE
before the Common Era. *See also* CE.

buttress
an architectural feature that is added to a building to help its walls support the weight of the roof.

ca. or circa
around or about. When we don't know the precise date of an event, we use the abbreviation "ca." For example, "ca. 360" means "around the year 360."

caliph
an Islamic ruler who claims to rule over all Muslims. In the Middle Ages, the caliph's empire was called the "caliphate."

catapult
a weapon used to hurl objects (like rocks) at castles and walls.

CE
of the Common Era. In the Middle Ages, Christians began counting time from the year they believed Jesus was born. Originally, dates were divided into "BC" (Before Christ) and "AD" (Anno Domini, or The Year of our Lord). Today, we use the terms "BCE" (Before the Common Era) and "CE" (of the Common Era).

church
a Christian place of worship.

diplomat
a person who visits the leaders of another country to build or maintain military and political alliances between the two countries.

emperor
a male ruler of a very large country or several countries.

empress
a female ruler of a very large country or several countries.

fermentation
the process of turning grains (like wheat), fruits (like grapes), or vegetables (like potatoes) into alcoholic drinks like beer, wine, or liquor.

fortress
a building with high stone walls designed to provide protection from military attacks. A castle is a kind of fortress.

furrier
a person who makes animal furs into clothes and goods

gristmill *See* mill.

guild
a formal association of workers who support each other and control the tools and trade connected with their craft.

imam
a spiritual leader in a Muslim community who leads prayers in the mosque.

infographic
an image that explains something using numbers or patterns. Examples of infographics include charts, graphs, maps, and diagrams.

journeyman
a craftsperson who has completed an apprenticeship and is working for a master craftsperson.

khan
a ruler of a Central Asian nomadic nation in the Middle Ages.

knight
a person who serves a king or queen in battle and is trained to fight from horseback.

lady
a noble woman.

lady-in-waiting
a noble woman who serves as a companion and assistant to a higher-ranking noble woman, princess, or queen.

linen
a type of cloth woven from the fibers of the flax plant.

lord
a noble man.

medieval
meaning "from the Middle Ages." The words come from the Latin *medius* for "middle" and *aevum* for "age."

merchant
a person who takes goods made by one person and sells them to another person.

midwife
a woman with specialized training to assist women through pregnancy and giving birth.

mihrab
a shallow recess in the wall of the mosque that indicates the direction of the holy city of Mecca, Saudi Arabia.

mill
a building that uses water or wind to make grain into flour by grinding it between two stones.

minaret
a tower connected to a mosque.

monarch
a ruler like a king, queen, emperor, or empress.

monk
a man who dedicates his life to the Christian religion and lives apart from the rest of society, often in a community of other monks.

monotheism
the belief that there is only one God.

mosque
a Muslim place of worship.

noble
a person of high rank in society.

nun
a woman who dedicates her life to the Christian religion and lives apart from the rest of society, often in a community of other nuns.

parchment
skin from a calf, sheep, or goat, processed to make it into a soft, thin material suitable for writing on.

patriarch
a senior leader in a Christian church, especially in Eastern Europe or the Byzantine empire.

patron
a person who financially supports the

career of an independent creative worker like an artist or writer.

peasant
a low-ranking person who lives on and farms a small plot of land in the countryside.

pilgrim
a person who goes on a journey (called a "pilgrimage") to visit a holy place.

plow
a tool used in farming to prepare the soil for planting.

polytheism
the belief that there are many gods.

pope
the head of the Catholic Church.

priest
a spiritual leader in a Christian community who gives sermons and is authorized to perform sacred rituals.

rabbi
a spiritual leader, scholar, and teacher within a Jewish community.

scribe
a person who makes a living by hand-copying documents and writing out new documents for others.

silk
a delicate fabric made from the cocoon of the larvae of some moths.

squire
a young person, often a boy, who carries a knight's shield and armor and trains to be a knight.

sultan
a ruler of an Islamic province or country.

synagogue
a Jewish place of worship.

tanner
a person who makes animal skins into clothes and leather goods.

textiles
fabrics.

vassal
a person who promises loyalty and support, including fighting in wartime, to a higher-ranking person in exchange for control over a plot of land.

weaver
a person who takes strands of thread or yarn and interlaces them to create cloth.

SELECTED BIBLIOGRAPHY

Benedictow, Ole Jørgen. *The Black Death, 1346–1353: The Complete History*. Woodbridge, UK: Boydell, 2004.

Davies, Norman. *Europe: A History*. Oxford: Oxford University Press, 1996.

Emery, Richard W. "The Black Death of 1348 in Perpignan." *Speculum* 42 (1967): 611–623.

Gies, Frances and Joseph. *Cathedral, Forge, and Waterwheel: Technology and Invention in the Middle Ages*. New York: HarperPerennial, 1995.

Gies, Frances and Joseph. *Daily Life in Medieval Times*. Rochester, UK: Grange, 2005.

Hanawalt, Barbara A. *Growing Up in Medieval London: The Experience of Childhood in History*. Oxford: Oxford University Press, 1993.

Hanawalt, Barbara A. *The Ties That Bound: Peasant Families in Medieval England*. Oxford: Oxford University Press, 1986.

Harvey, L.P. *Islamic Spain: 1250 to 1500*. Chicago: University of Chicago Press, 1993.

Herlihy, David. *Opera Muliebria: Women and Work in Medieval Europe*. New York: McGraw-Hill, 1990.

Mango, Cyril, ed. *The Oxford History of Byzantium*. Oxford: Oxford University Press, 2002.

"Marginalized." *Lapham's Quarterly* Spring 2012. Accessed at http://www.laphamsquarterly.org/visual/charts-graphs/marginalized.php (Feb. 14, 2013).

McEvedy, Colin. *The Penguin Atlas of Medieval History*. Harmondsworth, UK: Penguin, 1961.

McKitterick, Rosamond. *Atlas of the Medieval World*. New York: Oxford University Press, 2004.

Ohler, Norbert. *The Medieval Traveller*. Trans. Caroline Hillier. Woodbridge, UK: Boydell, 1989.

Oman, C.W.C. *The Art of War in the Middle Ages*. 1885. Ithaca: Cornell University Press, 1953.

Pounds, Norman. *An Economic History of Medieval Europe*. London: Longman, 1974.

Rawlings, Helen. *The Spanish Inquisition*. Malden: Blackwell, 2006.

Riley-Smith, Jonathan. *The Crusades: A Short History*. New Haven: Yale University Press, 1987.

Rossabi, Morris. *Voyager from Xanadu: Rabban Sauma and the First Journey from China to the West*. New York: Kodansha, 1992.

Stratford, Jenny. "The Early Royal Collections and the Royal Library to 1461." In *The Cambridge History of the Book in Britain*, vol. 3: *1400–1557*, ed. Lotte Hellinga and J.B. Trapp, 255–266. Cambridge: Cambridge University Press, 1999.

Trombert, Éric, and Étienne de la Vassière. "Les prix du marché à Turfan en 742." In *Études de Dunhuang et Turfan*, ed. J.-P. Drège, 1–52. Paris: EPHE-Droz, 2007.

INDEX